SCARY PLACES

Dark Labyrinths

by Michael E. Goodman

Consultant: Paul F. Johnston
Washington, D.C.

BEARPORT
PUBLISHING

New York, New York

Credits

Cover and Title Page, © Bliznetsov/Shutterstock, © Elena Yakusheva/Shutterstock, © Bart Kwieciszewski/Fotolia, and © Oleg Kozlov/iStockphoto; 4-5, © Paolo Siccardi/age fotostock; 6, © O. Louis Mazzatenta/NGS Image Collection; 7L, © Thomas Barrat/Shutterstock; 7R, © Dennis Cox/ChinaStock/WorldViews; 8, © Elena Yakusheva/Shutterstock; 9L, © P. Tomlins/Alamy; 9R, © Zeynep Mufti/Images&Stories; 10, © JTB Photo Communications, Inc./Alamy; 11L, © Richard Stead; 11R, © Henryk T. Kaiser/age fotostock; 12, © Tamas D. Varga/PanoGraph Ltd.; 13L, © Thomas Mueller/Alimdi; 13R, © Rainer Jahns; 14, © Museum of History & Industry, Seattle (MOHAI); 15, © Kelly-Mooney Photography/Corbis; 16, © Robert Harding Picture Library/SuperStock; 17, © Rue des Archives/The Granger Collection, New York; 18, © AP Images/David Zalubowski; 19L, © Courtesy U.S. Army Corps of Engineers; 19R, © Mark Richards/ZUMA Press; 20, © Kjell Sandved/Visuals Unlimited, Inc.; 21T, © Waitomo Museum of Caves; 21C, © Waitomo Museum of Caves; 21B, © Mark Taylor/BCIUSA/Photoshot; 22, © Sean Caffrey/Lonely Planet Images; 23L, © Nicolas Asfouri/AFP/Getty Images; 23R, © Herbert Barraud/Hulton Archive/Getty Images; 24, © Radius/SuperStock; 25L, © Stuart Pearce/World Pictures/Photoshot; 25R, Courtesy of The US Army; 26, © Andre Jenny/Alamy; 27L, © Reuters/Landov; 27R, © AP Images/U.S. Government/The Greenbrier; 31, © Pakhnyushcha/Shutterstock.

Publisher: Kenn Goin
Senior Editor: Lisa Wiseman
Creative Director: Spencer Brinker
Design: Dawn Beard Creative
Photo Researcher: Daniella Nilva

Library of Congress Cataloging-in-Publication Data

Goodman, Michael E.
  Dark labyrinths / by Michael Goodman.
      p. cm. — (Scary places)
  Includes bibliographical references and index.
  ISBN-13: 978-1-936087-56-3 (library binding)
  ISBN-10: 1-936087-56-1 (library binding)
  1. Labyrinths—Juvenile literature. I. Title.
  BL325.L3G66 2010
  725'.98—dc22

                              2009043582

For more information, write to Bearport Publishing Company, Inc., 101 Fifth Avenue, Suite 6R, New York, New York 10003. Printed in the United States of America in North Mankato, Minnesota.

122009
090309CGE

10 9 8 7 6 5 4 3 2 1

Contents

Dark Labyrinths

What's the most terrifying thing about being trapped in an underground **labyrinth**? Is it that there's no sunlight, making it nearly impossible to see what's lurking in the dark? Or is it the twists and turns of the tunnels, making it so easy to get lost? Perhaps it's the fear of running out of air. An underground room without oxygen could become a **tomb** in a matter of minutes.

No matter how forbidding these dark places are, people have used them throughout history—often, surprisingly, to stay safe. Among the 11 labyrinths in this book, you'll discover a church made of salt, pitch-black tunnels used for deadly sneak attacks, and a secret shelter designed to hide members of the U.S. Congress in case of **nuclear** war.

An Army Made of Clay

Xi'an, China

In 1974, there was almost no rain in Xi'an (SHEE-ahn). Crops were dying. Farmers knew the only way to save their farms was to dig a well to get water from the ground. Digging a well, however, terrified them. According to an old **legend**, there were ghosts hiding under the fields in Xi'an—the ghosts of ancient Chinese soldiers. In a strange way, the legend was right.

The terra-cotta soldiers

Desperate for water, the farmers of Xi'an began to dig a well, in spite of stories saying that the ground beneath them was haunted. They didn't find ghosts, however. What they found instead was a head and arm made out of terra-cotta, a kind of clay. When **archaeologists** heard about the discovery, they came to Xi'an and unearthed an entire underground palace with secret rooms connected by dark, winding tunnels. Some of the rooms were filled with life-size clay soldiers more than 2,000 years old.

Who had built the ancient labyrinth, and why? The archaeologists concluded that it had been created around 215 B.C. by Shi Huang (SHEE WONG), who became the first emperor of China at age 13. Although the young emperor was powerful, he was also afraid of death. As a result, he soon began building his own tomb. Over time, it would grow to become a sprawling underground city, complete with a clay army to stand guard and protect the emperor's spirit in the **afterlife**.

Emperor Shi Huang

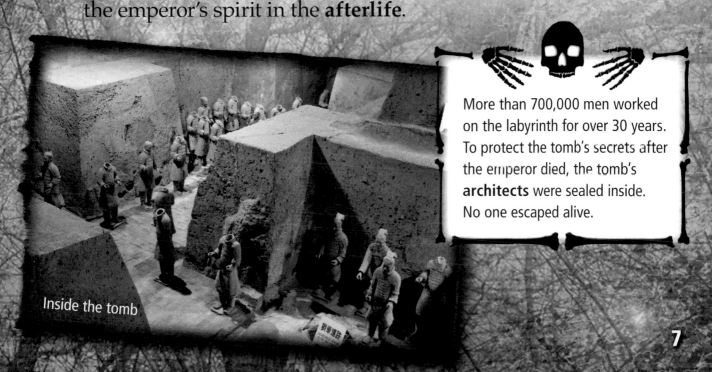

Inside the tomb

More than 700,000 men worked on the labyrinth for over 30 years. To protect the tomb's secrets after the emperor died, the tomb's **architects** were sealed inside. No one escaped alive.

A Place to Hide and Pray

Derinkuyu, Turkey

In 1963, a man knocking down a wall inside a cave in central Turkey made an amazing find. He discovered a huge underground city—Derinkuyu (*der*-in-KOO-yoo)—that had been forgotten for centuries. The city got its start more than 2,500 years ago, when people began to dig tunnel-like labyrinths in the soft layer of rock that lay below their towns. They hollowed out long hallways and secret rooms where they could hide when enemies attacked.

Derinkuyu

Over the centuries, as ancient townspeople continued to dig, the labyrinths of Derinkuyu became larger and larger—so large, in fact, that they came to form a small underground city. The city has 50 tunnels and its own river. Its longest passageway stretches 5.6 miles (9 km) and connects to another underground city, called Kaymakli.

Long ago, Derinkuyu had everything people needed to survive for months. Since parts of the city extended as deep as 278 feet (85 m) underground—the height of a 27-story building—its most important feature was a system of **ventilation shafts** that provided air from above. Beyond that, Derinkuyu also included kitchens, storage rooms, stables, and even schools and churches. Thick stone doors were used to seal off the entrance to each level of the city. Once they were in place, the people underground were safely hidden.

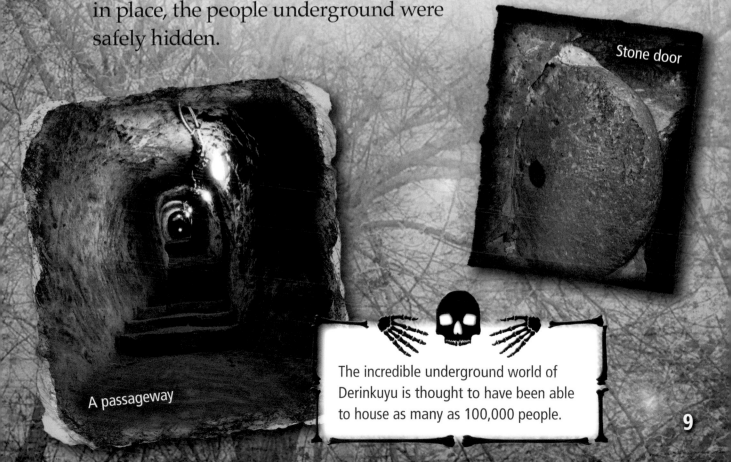

Stone door

A passageway

The incredible underground world of Derinkuyu is thought to have been able to house as many as 100,000 people.

Surrounded by Salt

Wieliczka, Poland

Before refrigerators, salt was used to keep food from spoiling. It was so valuable that it was known as white gold. The precious substance was produced either from seawater or from rock that had to be dug from deep within the earth. In Wieliczka (vee-LEETS-kuh), workers have been mining salt for more than 700 years. In that time, they have also created an eerie wonderland deep underground.

This photo shows what it was like to work in the salt mines.

The Wieliczka Salt Mine is massive, sprawling 186.4 miles (300 km) in length and extending as deep as 1,073 feet (327 m) belowground. It includes several underground lakes and nine levels of passageways, galleries, and chambers. One of the most amazing chambers is Saint Kinga's **Chapel**, which has been a place of worship since about 1896. Lit by huge **chandeliers** made with glass-like salt crystals, the chapel has an altar, statues, and detailed images carved from **rock salt**.

Three miners created the chapel over a period of 68 years. These underground workers needed places to pray, since theirs was a dangerous job. **Methane gas** builds up in mines and is easily ignited by a spark, a lamp, or other fire source. Daily, up to 2,000 workers in the Wieliczka Salt Mine faced the possibility of an explosion caused by this deadly gas.

Saint Kinga's Chapel

A passageway

According to legend, a ghost often appeared before disasters occurred in the Wieliczka Salt Mine and warned miners with the words "Do not go."

The Labyrinth of Courage

Budapest, Hungary

During World War II (1939–1945), Budapest (BOO-duh-*pest*) was invaded. German airplanes bombed the city. Russian tanks roared through the streets. Frightened people scattered during each attack, searching for safety. Thousands of them made their way to a hilly part of the city. There they entered the ancient labyrinth of Buda Castle, nicknamed the "Labyrinth of Courage," far belowground.

Inside the Labyrinth of Courage

The Labyrinth of Courage is millions of years old. It was created by rivers of hot water that pushed through layers of rock. The rushing water carved out a group of more than 200 tunnels, which underground workers later connected.

Long before World War II, people started using the tunnels as hiding places. In fact, scientists believe that cave dwellers may have been the first to do so, using the tunnels to escape from wild animals half a million years ago. Much later, after a bloody invasion by **Mongols** in the 13th century—the people of Hungary built Buda Castle on top of the labyrinth. The web of tunnels provided a place of safety for castle dwellers during times of battle. Finally, in the mid-twentieth century, the labyrinth became a shelter capable of housing 10,000 people—offering a place to escape from the violence and destruction of World War II.

Buda Castle

Today, people can tour the labyrinth, which is 4,000 feet (1,219 m) long. Using only oil lamps for light, visitors have to hold on to a rope to find their way through the pitch-black passages.

The entrance to the Labyrinth of Courage

Ghost Town Underground

Seattle, Washington

The neighborhood in Seattle called Pioneer Square was built on muddy, flat land. When the tide was very high in the nearby **inlet**, water often flooded the buildings. The sewers backed up, causing toilets to spew like fountains. Then, in 1889, a fire burned out of control and destroyed most of the structures in Pioneer Square. When the neighborhood was rebuilt, the builders accidentally created an underground ghost town.

Pioneer Square before the fire

The new streets of Pioneer Square were built between 12 feet (3.7 m) and 30 feet (9.1 m) higher than the old ones—to escape the mud and water damage caused by frequent floods. This meant that buildings not destroyed by the fire were now nearly hidden underground. This shadow town's remaining structures were connected by a winding labyrinth of dark, dirty streets. By 1907, most of the underground area was abandoned because of rats and disease. The people left, but some say ghosts have stayed behind.

Most of these spirits are the ghosts of people who had lived or worked in the area before the fire. One is a bank teller who nervously walks back and forth. People say he seems worried about all the gold he has to guard. Others tell of seeing a ghost sitting and staring sadly at the stage of an old theater. He had suffered a painful death when some stage lights fell on him during a play.

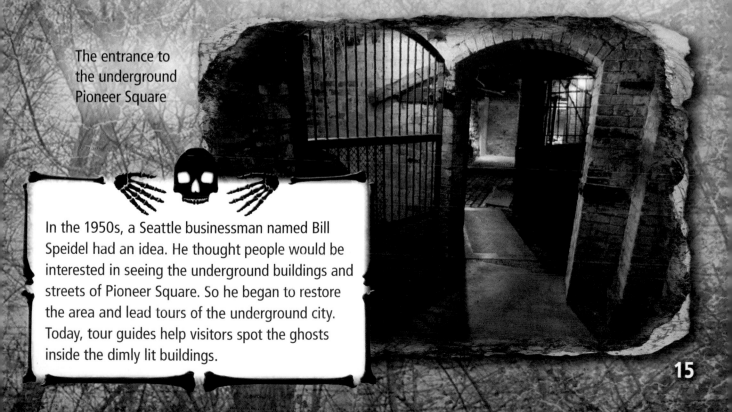

The entrance to the underground Pioneer Square

In the 1950s, a Seattle businessman named Bill Speidel had an idea. He thought people would be interested in seeing the underground buildings and streets of Pioneer Square. So he began to restore the area and lead tours of the underground city. Today, tour guides help visitors spot the ghosts inside the dimly lit buildings.

The Secret Subway

Moscow, Russia

Every day, people who live in the city of Moscow (MOS-kow) take the Metro to work. It's the busiest subway system in the world. Little do many of them know, the Metro may not be Moscow's only subway system. Though the government denies its existence, a mystery subway, the Metro 2, is said to exist 164 to 656 feet (50 to 200 m) belowground. Why is this labyrinth such a big secret?

The Moscow Metro

If accounts about Moscow's secret subway are true, work on Metro 2 began during World War II, when German troops were marching toward Moscow. During this time of great fear, the Soviet Union's powerful leader, Joseph Stalin, thought about destroying the Metro so the Germans couldn't capture and use it. However, he changed his mind and kept the trains running. Then—according to reports—he ordered a secret labyrinth to be dug far below the original Metro. He planned to build a hidden subway system there to take Soviet leaders outside of Moscow in case the Germans captured the city.

In the early 1950s, Stalin would have had another purpose for Metro 2. It would serve as a bomb shelter if nuclear war broke out between his country and the United States. Supposedly, work on Metro 2 stopped after Stalin died in 1953, but some of the tunnels are still around, locked away and hidden. As far as most people know, Metro 2 has never been finished and was never used for train travel.

If Metro 2 indeed exists, most of the workers who built it must have been women. Why? Most of the city's men were in the Soviet army, fighting in World War II.

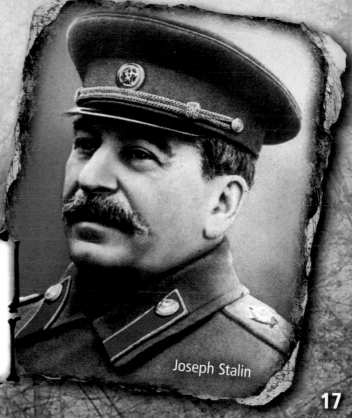

Joseph Stalin

America's Fortress

Colorado Springs, Colorado

In a human-made labyrinth 2,000 feet (610 m) inside a Colorado mountain, government workers scan computer screens day and night. **Satellites** that track everything that moves through Earth's skies beam information to computers inside the mountain's labyrinth 24 hours a day, 7 days a week. If something flashes across the screens, the operators have to quickly decide whether or not it poses a threat. If it does, they must act quickly, or millions of U.S. citizens may die.

The entrance to Cheyenne Mountain

CHEYENNE MOUNTAIN COMPLEX

INSIDE THE
MOUNTAIN
IS A
NO HAT
NO SALUTE
AREA

The labyrinth inside Cheyenne (shy-EHN) Mountain was built in the 1960s to help the United States survive a nuclear war. The entrance has two 25-ton (23-metric-ton) doors. They are so well made that even though they're very heavy, only two people are needed to push them open. Inside the mountain, there are 15 buildings set on more than 1,000 springs. The springs will prevent the buildings from collapsing if the labyrinth is hit by earthquakes or nuclear explosions. The operation center can withstand a 30-**megaton** bomb blast. Water is provided by 1.5-million-gallon (5.7-million-liter) underground **reservoirs** that are so large, it takes a rowboat to cross them.

The computer system in the labyrinth is set up to warn the U.S. Air Force of enemy missile attacks. When the computers show something in the air, operators must quickly determine if it is "space junk" moving through the sky or if America is under attack.

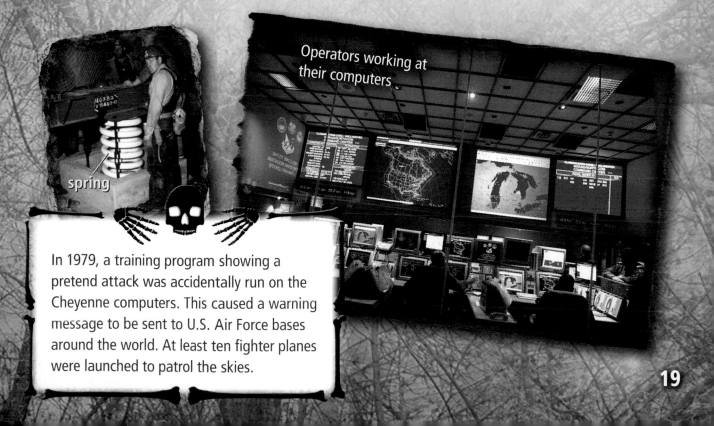

spring

Operators working at their computers

In 1979, a training program showing a pretend attack was accidentally run on the Cheyenne computers. This caused a warning message to be sent to U.S. Air Force bases around the world. At least ten fighter planes were launched to patrol the skies.

The Worms Crawl In

Waitomo, New Zealand

For nearly a thousand years, the **Maori** people of New Zealand told stories about glittering "stars" shining inside an underground cave. This legendary place was called Waitomo (whye-TOH-moh), which means "water hole" in the Maori language. The only known way to enter Waitomo was through an underground stream that flowed from one pitch-black tunnel to another. Who would brave the darkness for a chance to reach the stars?

Inside Waitomo

In 1887, a Maori chief named Tane Tinorau (TAH-nay TIN-or-oo) and a British man named Fred Mace decided to paddle into Waitomo. They built a small raft out of reeds, a type of tall grass. They passed through several dark tunnels and then entered an open underground room. Its low ceiling was covered with tiny lights. They put out their torches and reached up to the ceiling to touch the "stars." That's when they discovered the secret of Waitomo.

Tane Tinorau

The lights were actually thousands of glowworms! These little creatures give off a soft blue light to attract the bugs they eat. The explorers backed out of the room carefully and paddled out to tell others what they had found. Today, descendants of Tane Tinorau guide visitors through the dripping caverns, filled with oozing **stalactites** and **stalagmites**.

Fred Mace

stalactites

stalagmites

The glowworms are not the only special feature of the caves. The largest room inside, called "the Cathedral," has great **acoustics**. That means it is an excellent place to perform or hear music. Several famous singers have come to Waitomo to fill the dimly lit caves with beautiful music.

21

Ghosts in the Tube

London, England

The world's first subway system, the "Tube," opened in London in 1863. The idea of building anything underground frightened some people at the time. A minister in one London church warned it would allow the devil to escape from the underworld. Since the Tube was built, no one has seen the devil below London. However, some people say they have seen ghosts.

The Tube today

In the nearly 150 years since it opened, many people have died in the Tube, also known as the London Underground. Trains have crashed, people have been murdered, fires have broken out, and stations have been bombed. Plus, while workers dug the tunnels, many graves were disturbed. The Aldgate Tube station, for example, was built in the middle of a mass grave where 1,000 people were buried during the **plague** of 1665.

It's no wonder that ghosts have been seen in many of the stations. Some people claim that the ghost of a dead actress still performs in Aldwych station, where a theater once stood. Another station, Covent Garden, is said to be haunted by the actor William "Breezy Bill" Terriss, who was stabbed to death nearby in 1897. As he lay dying, he was heard to say, "I'll be back." Since then, Breezy Bill has been spotted in a gray suit and white gloves, waiting for the train.

William "Breezy Bill" Terriss

An abandoned Aldwych station

Not all ghosts that haunt the Tube are people. In 1928, a passenger on a train passing through South Kensington station heard a loud, piercing train whistle. He then watched an entire "ghost train" disappear right in front of him.

23

Tunnel Rats

Cu Chi, Vietnam

During the 1960s, the United States took part in the Vietnam War (1957–1975) in North Vietnam. Some of the strangest and scariest fighting during that war took place in dark, narrow tunnels near the city of Cu Chi (KOO CHEE). The American soldiers who risked their lives in the Cu Chi labyrinths proudly called themselves "tunnel rats." Like rats, the soldiers were relatively small and could be quite dangerous—and they hunted in the dark.

An entrance to a "rat" tunnel

Tunnel rats had more to worry about than just the enemy. The tunnels were often booby-trapped with bamboo spikes. Also, many of the tunnels were infested with ants, poisonous centipedes, spiders, snakes, and mosquitoes.

During the Vietnam War, many Americans were killed during surprise raids. The enemy soldiers seemed to come out of nowhere, like ghosts, and then disappear after they attacked. In time, the Americans discovered that their deadly enemies were living inside a **network** of tunnels that were up to 120 miles (193 km) long. The only way to stop the surprise raids was to invade these labyrinths.

The tunnel rats who took on this job had to be less than five feet six inches (1.7 m) tall to squeeze through the narrow, pitch-black **maze**. They carried only small weapons and flashlights, and wore kneepads because they often had to make their way through the tunnels on their knees. The rats seldom fired their guns underground. The noise from a gun blast in a tunnel could burst a person's eardrums. Instead, they fought with knives or their hands. Remembering these underground battles, some tunnel rats had nightmares for a long time after the war.

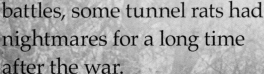
Inside a tunnel

A soldier being helped into a tunnel

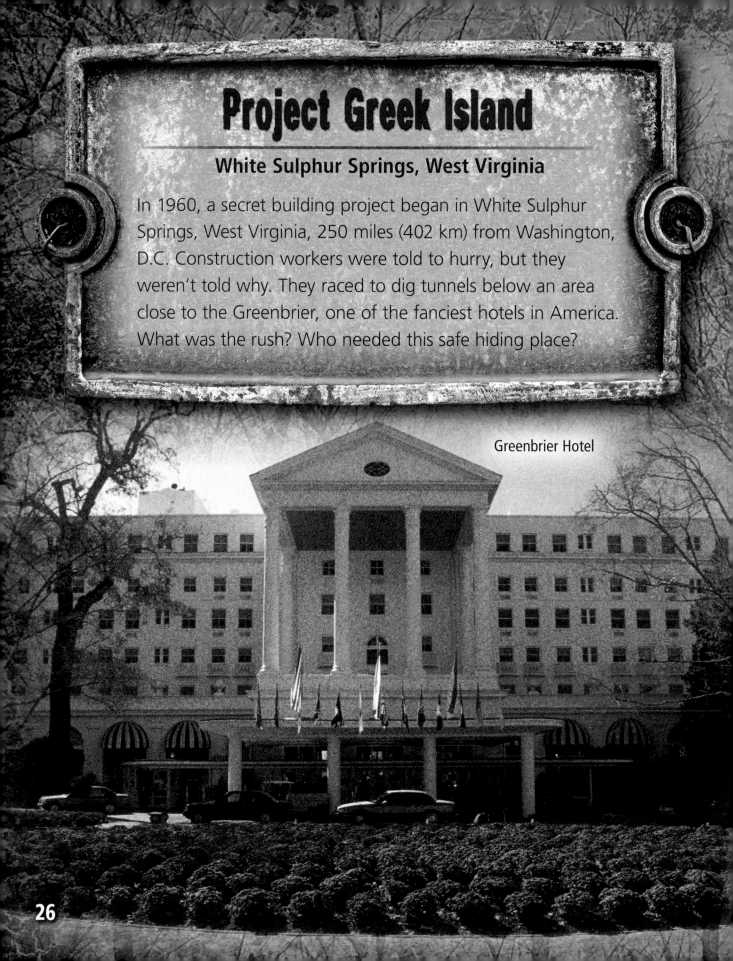

Project Greek Island

White Sulphur Springs, West Virginia

In 1960, a secret building project began in White Sulphur Springs, West Virginia, 250 miles (402 km) from Washington, D.C. Construction workers were told to hurry, but they weren't told why. They raced to dig tunnels below an area close to the Greenbrier, one of the fanciest hotels in America. What was the rush? Who needed this safe hiding place?

Greenbrier Hotel

The reason for the labyrinth near the Greenbrier Hotel was kept secret for more than 30 years. Most hotel workers didn't even know that it existed. Then, in 1992, a newspaper reporter revealed the truth about "Project Greek Island," the official name for the secret project. The tunnels were built to be a shelter for members of the U.S. Congress in case a nuclear attack was made on Washington.

Why West Virginia? Nearby mountains made it hard to attack by plane. Also, strong winds in the area could blow away any poisonous gases caused by a nuclear bomb. Food, water, air tanks, and **generators** were stored inside the shelter in case members of Congress needed to stay underground for a long time. There were medical offices, dental offices—even a place to **cremate** bodies. After the newspaper story was printed, the government decided to end any plans of using the secret shelter.

Paul Bugas

The labyrinth being built

Paul Bugas was one of many Greenbrier employees leading a double life. Part of the time, he ran the television repair crew at the Greenbrier Hotel. He was also secretly in charge of maintaining the Congressional television station in the labyrinth.

27

Wieliczka, Poland

A massive salt mine with magnificent chandeliers

London, England

Ghosts wait at many of the city's subway stations

White Sulphur Springs, West Virginia

A secret labyrinth built to house members of the U.S. Congress during a nuclear attack

NORTH AMERICA

EUROPE

AFRICA

Seattle, Washington

An abandoned underground neighborhood

Colorado Springs, Colorado

A human-made labyrinth where government workers are on the lookout for attacks against the United States

SOUTH AMERICA

Budapest, Hungary

An underground hiding place for people during World War II

Pacific Ocean

Atlantic Ocean

N

W   E

S

Southern Ocean

Around the World

ASIA

Moscow, Russia

A secret subway system that may or may not exist

Xi'an, China

Clay soldiers protect a long-dead emperor in an underground palace

Cu Chi, Vietnam

Soldiers hunt the enemy in maze-like tunnels

*Indian
Ocean*

*Pacific
Ocean*

Derinkuyu, Turkey

An underground city filled with all the necessities for living belowground

AUSTRALIA

Waitomo, New Zealand

Thousands of glowworms light up a room in a cave

ANTARCTICA

Glossary

acoustics (uh-KOO-stiks) how well sound can be carried or heard in a room

afterlife (AF-tur-*life*) a person's existence after he or she has died

archaeologists (*ar*-kee-OL-uh-jists) scientists who learn about ancient times by studying things they dig up, such as old buildings and tools

architects (AR-ki-tekts) people who design buildings and make sure they are built properly

chandeliers (*shan*-duh-LIHRZ) fancy light fixtures that hang from ceilings

chapel (CHAP-uhl) a building or room used for praying

cremate (KREE-mayt) to burn a dead body to ashes

generators (JEN-uh-*ray*-tuhrz) devices used to make electrical energy

inlet (IN-let) a narrow body of water running from a larger body of water, such as an ocean, into land

labyrinth (LAB-*uh*-rinth) a set of winding, connected pathways in which it is easy to get lost

legend (LEJ-uhnd) a story handed down from long ago that is often based on some facts but cannot be proven true

Maori (MAH-oh-ree) the native people of New Zealand

maze (MAYZ) a confusing group of paths that is set up like a puzzle

megaton (MEG-*uh*-tuhn) the explosive force of one million tons (907,185 metric tons) of dynamite

methane gas (METH-ayn GASS) a colorless, odorless, flammable gas often found in mines

Mongols (MON-guhlz) people from the Mongol Empire, which stretched through Asia and parts of Europe during the 1200s and 1300s

network (NET-*wurk*) a group of parts joined together, such as a group of buildings or tunnels

nuclear (NOO-klee-ur) having to do with a type of energy that is produced by splitting atoms

plague (PLAYG) a disease that spreads quickly and often kills many people

reservoirs (REZ-ur-*vwarz*) natural or artificial holding areas for storing water

rock salt (ROK SAWLT) salt found in solid form as a mineral

satellites (SAT-uh-lites) spacecraft that are sent into outer space to gather and send back information to Earth

stalactites (stuh-LAK-*tites*) icicle-shaped mineral deposits that hang from the roof of a cave

stalagmites (stuh-LAG-*mites*) cone-shaped mineral deposits that build up on the floor of a cave

tomb (TOOM) a grave, room, or building designed to house a dead body

ventilation shafts (*ven*-tuh-LAY-shuhn SHAFTS) passageways that allow fresh air into an area and stale air out

Bibliography

Fischler, Stan. *Subways of the World.* Osceola, WI: MBI Publishing (2000).

Mangold, Tom, and John Penycate. *The Tunnels of Cu Chi.* New York: Random House (1985).

Marshall, Alex. *Beneath the Metropolis: The Secret Lives of Cities.* New York: Carroll & Graf (2006).

Mooney, Paul, Catherine Maudsley, and Gerald Hatherly. *Xi'an, Shaanxi, and the Terracotta Army.* Hong Kong: Odyssey Publications (2005).

Smith, Stephen. *Underground London: Travels Beneath the City Streets.* London: Little, Brown (2004).

Westwood, Jennifer, ed. *The Atlas of Mysterious Places: The World's Unexplained Sacred Sites, Symbolic Landscapes, Ancient Cities, and Lost Lands.* New York: Grove Press (1987).

Read More

Pascoe, Elaine. *The London Underground.* San Diego, CA: Blackbirch Press (2004).

Prior, Natalie Jane. *Caves, Graves, and Catacombs: Secrets from Beneath the Earth.* London: Allen & Unwin (1996).

Learn More Online

To learn more about dark labyrinths, visit
www.bearportpublishing.com/ScaryPlaces

Index

About the Author

Michael E. Goodman is a writer and editor who lives above
the ground in New Jersey. He has written dozens of books for
children about interesting people and places.